# Bugs

# Weta

by Trudy Becker

FOCUS
READERS®

PIONEER

# www.focusreaders.com

Focus Readers is distributed by North Star Editions: sales@northstareditions.com | 888-417-0195

Produced for Focus Readers by Red Line Editorial.

Photographs ©: Shutterstock Images, cover, 1, 6, 10, 14, 18, 20; iStockphoto, 4, 8, 17; Chris Winks/Wikimedia, 12

**Library of Congress Cataloging-in-Publication Data**
Names: Becker, Trudy, author.
Title: Weta / by Trudy Becker.
Description: Lake Elmo, MN : Focus Readers, 2023. | Series: Bugs | Includes
    index. | Audience: Grades 2-3
Identifiers: LCCN 2022035861 (print) | LCCN 2022035862 (ebook) | ISBN
    9781637394540 (hardcover) | ISBN 9781637394915 (paperback) | ISBN
    9781637395646 (pdf) | ISBN 9781637395288 (ebook)
Subjects: LCSH: Wetas--Juvenile literature.
Classification: LCC QL506 .B43 2023  (print) | LCC QL506  (ebook) | DDC
    595.7/26--dc23/eng/20220818
LC record available at https://lccn.loc.gov/2022035861
LC ebook record available at https://lccn.loc.gov/2022035862

Printed in the United States of America
Mankato, MN
012023

# About the Author

Trudy Becker lives in Minneapolis, Minnesota. She likes exploring new places and loves anything involving books.

# Table of Contents

# Chapter 1

# Out of Sight

The sun is going down. Night is coming. A weta crawls out of a hole. It was hiding all day. But now it's time to move.

Weta are insects. There are many different types of weta. They all live in New Zealand. Some live in trees. Some live in caves. And some live on the ground.

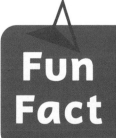

# Chapter 2

# Weta Bodies

A weta has six legs. It also has three main body parts. It has a head. It has a **thorax** in the middle. And it has an **abdomen** at the back.

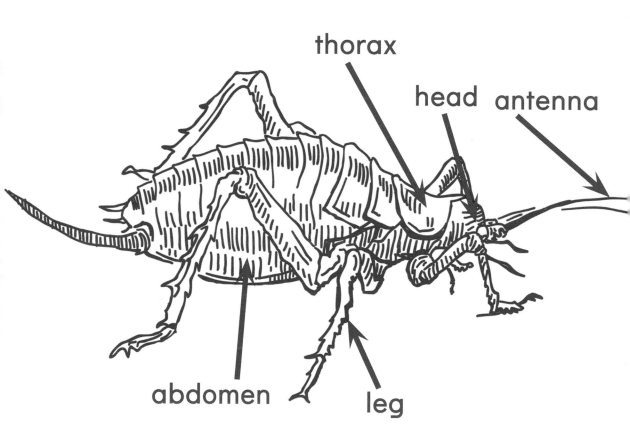

thorax

head    antenna

abdomen    leg

All weta have **antennae** to sense things. But not all weta look the same. They are different sizes. Some have long, thin antennae. Other weta have strong legs for jumping far.

**Fun Fact**

Weta have ears behind their knees.

# Chapter 3

# Weta Strengths

Some weta have **tusks**. The tusks come out of their jaws. But the tusks aren't for biting. Weta use them to fight. They push their enemies with the tusks.

If weta are in danger, they try to defend themselves. They can stretch their back legs. They show their spines. That scares or scratches **predators**.

**Fun Fact** Giant weta are the biggest kind of weta. They can weigh more than mice.

# Rat Danger

In the past, weta did not have many predators. But then, rats came to their **habitats**. Rats can easily smell weta. Rats hunt them. Now, some weta are **endangered**. People are trying to help. They make safe areas where weta can live.

# Weta Life

Weta eat lots of different foods. Many are **omnivores**. Some weta eat insects. Many weta eat leaves. Other weta can eat fruit or seeds. Giant weta eat carrots, too.

ovipositor

Female weta have parts called **ovipositors**. They use them to lay eggs. Weta put eggs deep in the soil. Later, the eggs hatch. It can take two years for an egg to grow into an adult.

**Fun Fact**

Many weta live in holes or tunnels.

# FOCUS ON
# Weta

*Write your answers on a separate piece of paper.*

1. Write a sentence that explains the main idea of Chapter 4.

2. Weta live in New Zealand. What insects live near your home?

3. What is the middle part of a weta's body?
   - A. wing
   - B. abdomen
   - C. thorax

4. Why is soil a safe place for weta to lay eggs?
   - A. Soil makes the eggs taste bad.
   - B. Soil hides the eggs from predators.
   - C. Predators are afraid of soil.

*Answer key on page 24.*

# Glossary

**abdomen**
The back part of an insect. It contains the heart and stomach.

**antennae**
Long, thin body parts on an insect's head. The parts are used for sensing.

**endangered**
In danger of dying out.

**habitats**
Places where animals live.

**omnivores**
Animals that eat both meat and plants to survive.

**ovipositors**
Body parts used by female insects to lay eggs.

**predators**
Animals that hunt other animals for food.

**thorax**
The middle part of an insect. The legs are attached to this part.

**tusks**
Long, pointed teeth that stick out from the faces of some animals.

# To Learn More

## BOOKS

Levy, Janey. *Giant Wetas Shock!* New York: Gareth Stevens Publishing, 2018.

Schuh, Mari. *Cricket or Grasshopper?* Minneapolis: Bellwether Media, 2022.

## NOTE TO EDUCATORS

Visit **www.focusreaders.com** to find lesson plans, activities, links, and other resources related to this title.

# Index

**Answer Key: 1.** Answers will vary; **2.** Answers will vary; **3.** C; **4.** B